Davie Street Translations

DAVIE STREET TRANSLATIONS

Daniel Zomparelli

Talonbooks

Talonbooks
P.O. Box 2076, Vancouver, British Columbia, Canada V6B 3S3
www.talonbooks.com

Typeset in Adobe Jenson and PID Kuhrier.
Printed and bound in Canada on acid-free, SFI-certified paper.
Typeset by Typesmith. Cover design by Easton West.

First printing: 2012

The publisher gratefully acknowledges the financial support of the Canada Council
for the Arts, the Government of Canada through the Canada Book Fund and the
Province of British Columbia through the British Columbia Arts Council and the Book
Publishing Tax Credit for our publishing activities.

Library and Archives Canada Cataloguing in Publication

Zomparelli, Daniel, 1985–
    Davie Street translations / Daniel Zomparelli.

Poems.
ISBN 978-0-88922-683-8

    I. Title.

PS8649.O66D38 2012   C811'.6   C2012-900022-1

Acknowledgements

Much gratitude to Garry Thomas Morse and Greg Gibson for their editing magic and wisdom.

Thank you to Billeh Nickerson for helping me through second and third edits of an earlier version of the manuscript and for having all of our meetings at the Pumpjack.

Thank you for your friendship and support in producing this manuscript, Lauren Bercovitch, Sean Condon, Ivan Coyote, Brad Cran, Morgan Brayton, Dave Deveau, Elee Kraljii Gardiner, Brandon Gaukel, Gillian Jerome, Alex Leslie, Leah Rae, Nikki Reimer, Rachel Rose, Rob Seebacher, Easton West and whoever I have missed.

Thank you to the editors of *Branch*, *CV2*, *EVENT*, *Feathertale*, *OCW Magazine*, *subTerrain*, *White Rabbit Quarterly* and *V6A: Writing from Vancouver's Downtown Eastside* for printing earlier versions of these poems.

Thank you to my family for the reason I rely on humour so heavily.

A special thanks to Maja Miljkovic for listening to me rant about poetics when she really couldn't give a shit and for taking care of me when I couldn't. I love you. And thanks to all of my friends I didn't have space to mention.

Thank you to everyone who told me their stories and for being inspirational, including Isolde N. Barron, Raye Sunshine, Jaylene Tyme and Vera Way.

Thank you, Mom, I miss you.

And thank you, for reading this book.

Vancouver Sunrise

Sun rises
over city.

Take newspaper
off its shelf.

Skim over
gangbangers.

Skip to cross-
word puzzle

and there is a four-letter
word for precipitation.

I Could Teach This to the Young

SkyTrain to Waterfront – faces reflected impassive as in an
old T.S. Eliot poem – as if the set of the face belied the interior
mind – and it does – try it – I could teach this to the young.
— GEORGE STANLEY, *Vancouver: A Poem*

I sit next to a row of senior men, one drops his
hat and I place it back on his chair.
He
thanks me and his friend whispers, *I think*
he wanted to give you more than your hat back. They snicker
as old men do. I take my seat behind them
and they carry on about how one of their friends has
resorted to duct tape to remove all of his body hair.
One suggests a sex act and it moves on to
double-sided tape, which proves age does not
decay our appreciation of a "double-sided" joke. I make my way from
SkyTrain to Waterfront – faces reflected impassive as in an

old zombie movie. iPods in place, they can't hear
that one is in the way of the other, so they bump and
grimace their way through the seats. As I shuffle my
music I think back to the three men in the coffee shop.

They cobbled over talks of Madonna, iPods, Lady Gaga
and the days of disco. I can recall an
old T.S. Eliot poem – as if the set of the face belied the interior

but what will *we* discuss when
faces grow long and peaches are eaten.
Duct tape that
thought.
Is this all we have: a joke, a snicker and a hat thrown in?
Does George Stanley
talk about Lady Gaga as well? Does he
duct tape his body clean? Try to turn
your brain away from older men and
duct tape and the thought runs right
back into your dirty
mind – and it does – try it – I could teach this to the young.

Faded

Drank your outfit on, drank the
walk to Celebrities, drank to
Odyssey, but you drank a sailor
outfit for this invite only

and drank your way out of embarr-
assment, drank your way into tongue
the bartender at Numbers in your cell-
phone, drank your way into

Pumpjack, drank your way
into bathroom-stall latex sex, drank
your way into Denny's, drank your
way into his home, drank your way

into sleep, drank tears, drank into your
car, drank your way home, drank your sleep
drank your ass out of bed, drank the
morning, drank forgotten, drank you.

Grindr

It's 2 a.m., when attentions
are erect and the chance for new play
dwindles as the club empties out. It's
hard on the brain to get off the things
you want to do, but with the right
bad intentions, the right moment comes
with the wrong guy. So it has come to this
so it has cum to this. Call me up
on the line, and meet me late at
night, lusting, hungry and hung –
retell the same old tale, same old tail
and find yourself on a familiar bed
just remember that the walk of shame
tastes different when it's not the same.
      When you're the one to blame.
      Ain't that a shame.

A Part of Your World

for Vera Way

Fins for feet when you know you are something
more. *I would be beautiful, I would be beautiful.*
Vera Way from those in black dresses.
Vera will make you a spot of tea, with hair
like mother before the night runs. Watch
the 1960s sink into your arms. Shed fins
like shed gender, like the dick slips off
with a kick and a spin. A whole new world
of drag, she can't be stopped. No gut, no
beer in hand, no beard under a wig. So
she fell prey to a woman in a black dress
selling relationships for a career in singing.
Wouldn't you? *He would love me.* Don't worry
if you lose your voice, you can always lip-synch.

for Isolde N. Barron

I first met you, sitting at a windowsill
Celine Dion smile so that I couldn't understand
anything you were saying. *Love* sounds like *lurve*
and *heart* like *hurt*. I should have known you
would steal her voice, when you pulled on
black dress, and skin purpled like held breath.
You were surrounded by so many men
who couldn't remember their own names
or how they got to the Cobalt so late at night
like fish in a sea too dark to see a thought.
I was not upset you stole her voice, poor
unfortunate soul, she was just looking
for a man in a different pool, as we all are.
We all search for husbands under the sea.

French Toast

You put your nose close to
the glass when no one is looking
smell, tingle of
nostrils lets forth a sneeze,

as ninety dollars' worth of drugs fall
over the couch,
back away and make a joke
about how pillows look like French toast
when freshly dusted with powder.

So It Is Written

he claims to be straight but when he's drunk enough he
calls me and this is where we fuck.
– written in a men's bathroom stall at The Bay,
downtown Vancouver

It is written on the walls, of
the bathroom stalls, it is
felt-penned, scratched, etched
burnt onto the linoleum.

If bathroom stalls could talk
they would probably say, *he claims to be straight*
but when he's drunk enough
he calls me and this is where we fuck.

If you keep it on the DL
there is no closet necessary
because bathroom stalls
suffice just the same.

Break them down, one
by one. Start with the door
unhinge the rest until all
that is left is a toilet seat.

True Story

Your ex-boyfriend slept
with your boyfriend's ex-
boyfriend's ex-boyfriend
the night he partied with
his ex-boyfriend and you.

Your boyfriend's ex-
boyfriend never gave up on
your boyfriend so he tried
to sleep with you. Now his
ex-boyfriend messaged your
boyfriend under another name.

Your friend's ex-boyfriend
is your ex-boyfriend who
dated your other ex-boyfriend
but is still in love with you.

Your ex-boyfriend's ex-
boyfriend's ex-boyfriend's ex-
boyfriend is you.

Take a Picture of Yourself in Your Underwear

rules, for everyone

Wear Gucci and H&M,
      don't go to the Fountainhead,
            wear red, not green.

            Take a picture of yourself
      in your underwear.
Don't iPhone, use BlackBerry,

it's Blenz not Starbucks.
      Smoothies, not protein shakes,
            no one talks to him anymore.

            Don't talk to the D's.
      He's not that attractive,
but he's smart, always keep one.

Don't worry if you're not attractive,
      working out fixes that. By the way,
            click a pic of yourself in briefs.

            Third Beach, stay on the left side.
      At this point I'm not sure why you are still using
gel. No beer, it's vodka on the rocks.

American Apparel is not even last year.
      Which reminds me, take a picture
            of yourself in your underwear.

            We only go to the clubs after midnight,
      don't pay cover, use the left
bar. Your picture, underwear.

Never bring cheap beer
      to a Yaletown party, that's
            not the right haircut.

Hamburger Mary's

It's 2 a.m. and you can barely put
a string of words together, bust a gut
      at the guy passed out on the booth. You were
      dancing on him a few hours before. Sure
his heart melts like cheese in your burger
but he can unbutton your jeans with a sure
      smile. Last night you two moved the beach
      ten feet from the shore, spent each
other's eyes on a future and left
all the seamen adrift
      in the sand. It's not like you were really
      in love, just playing pretend, silly
like you did in school. But now
it's 2 a.m. and there's gravy on his brow
      so reality has shadowed the mood
      and your burger is better than it should
be, which means it's not veggie like
you had ordered. Bike
      home and cry as you find it so lonely
      here. Maybe it's just the city
and maybe it's just your anxiety. You would
move to a small town, but it could
      be dangerous for a homo like you. Just
      remember when you throw up what
is possibly the meat patty you just ate
that it's not the booze or the feeling of it being too late.

Rapid HIV Testing

All in sixty seconds
sweat life out of skin
with just a bit of blood you
remember the bad decision and
should have worn protection
when you
let passion push out logic
in a single moment.
Can you recall the sexual partners
of the nights before?
Here are the results.

Here are the results
of the nights before.
Can you recall the sexual partners
in a single moment?
Let passion push out logic
when you
should have worn protection
remember the bad decision and
with just a bit of blood you
sweat life out of skin.
All in sixty seconds.

Monster

Sticky coffee hands, the time
you waited for him outside his place, stalking
                    isn't what it was – lust.
                            Wait and
            hope the lingering stares
            of men are permanent
Line up, your best shirt,
            hope no one in your family sees
don't
give a shit attitude
                glitter
because you're a proud to
            be here queer.
Music
blasts
you have a *yeah, I'm*
                    a homo, but I don't
                    identify as gay attitude.
Bump DMX mouth
            the word *faggot* as he
barks
            Stop buy the Junction, the
                        junction function
putting together men, pump
            jacked up for the
next party
            theme.
Sticky coffee hands
            hope the lingering stares
            of men are permanent
leave the car at Toyota
            slip into Odyssey for free
                    where we
blind the one-eyed monster.

GPS

By car
head north on Gladys Ave.
take first right onto BC-11 / Sumas Way
take the Trans-Canada to Vancouver
Exit 26 left at Hwy 7A / Hastings St. E.
continue to Howe
turn right on Davie
by iron rod
beat head
hit over shoulder
slightly to the left
knock unconscious

PLEASE
TO AVOID

DAVIE ST 110

it you wish to go

AD THE FOLLOWING
FUSION OR CONFLICT

HEAD

CIGARS
stogies
FAGS cuban
tobacco
SORRY NO WEED

SLIPPERY

MUSHROOMS

OR OT GAY

H WOULD

STAND PIPE
ONNECTION

beer is an art

$8.45 $7.5

PUMPJACK PUI

Pumpjack

Do you think this is what we'll look like?
    What?
        When we're old.
            I guess.
Do you think we'll be into ball gags?
    I think it's a matter of taste.
        I don't know. I'm kind of already into
            leather. I just bought a leather vest.

Last week I took it out
    The vest?
        and wore it around the room –
        my tits got sweaty.
What about rubber?
    Yeah, I can't see myself wanting to be suffocated in a rubber suit.
        What about fisting?
        Golden showers?
I think we'll get bored.
    I think we'll just get more and more kinky.
        Yeah, like, first a little slap, then a pinch, then butt plug.
        Won't we just be into antiquing by then?
Do you think this is what we'll look like?
    What?
        When we're old.
             I guess.

Another Sex Dream

from the street, each deserving man
would approach for a taste of this
transformation, so by dawn, I'd be raw
and then, by evening, ready and healed.
— MICHAEL V. SMITH, "Salvation"

I keep having sex dreams
of all men. Men of age, colour, time,
travel and work. My sixty-seven-year-
old boss, my thirty-two-year-old boss
my Muslim co-worker, my
friends, men I don't even know
and a few women with manly haircuts
for good measure and I
pull them
from the street, each deserving man

could feel the warmth and they
cry tears. Cry love, cry semen, cry
goodbyes and *not-this-time*s. They have never
been so pleased. I am a machine
of pleasure, a Fleshlight of hope. Like
a Madonna video, but with fewer feathers.
Like an endless tequila bottle, enough
to go around. I would
be Lil' Kim, so that everyone
would approach for a taste of this

and l-l-l-l-l-lick me from my head
to my toes. They would lie back
satiated, and even though
I find them
in their self-loathing, I go back for more.
I go back, even though my heart is a brick
even though they don't love me
even though this is not for me.
I go until there is a
transformation, so by dawn, I'd be raw

and be tired in my right arm. I used to wonder
why the hell I have sex
dreams against my will, but I traced it
back to Catholic guilt. Like Miss USA, I hope
for world peace, and I can
do that with my mouth. That
the broken men could cry to release
so that I take their pain
and the world can hurt in the morning
and then, by evening, ready and healed.

Icing or Sprinkles or Candy

Cocaine like haikus doesn't have enough lines to get me through the winter.

He took a line there said *wooweeee* and started to twirl, skip away from it all.

It's forty dollars, do you have a key to use? Use the bathroom.

What's your name again? Daniel. *Darryl?* Dan-iel ... fuck it. Yes: Darryl.

There's a pile up there. I'm falling asleep again, wake me when we go.

I love being broke. Everyone is nice to you offering free lines.

You've got something on your nose ... and your pants ... and your shirt.

Where did you get this dime bag? You bought it. *Oh, yeah.*

Growing Nails

When you were told his hobby
was growing his nails, you laughed
but his earnest face made you question
what he was on. When you saw him dripping
sweat from dancing, it was then you noticed
how short your nails were.

It's Taut

In 2008, three-quarters of crimes related to sexual orientation were violent ... Men were the victims in 85 per cent of violent cases linked to sexual orientation.
– Globe and Mail

We move out from
the club, sweat drips
and men gather.
Hear them chuckle

Why don't you fags
come suck these cocks.
We move. Silence
knowing what eight

men could do to
four faggots. One
follows behind
and throats a

fake laugh and we
move into the
7-Eleven.
They wait for

us outside the
store and we walk
out ignoring fear.
They jump the largest

of us, thinking
topple the giant
then get the rest.
We pull them off

and continue
to punch, blood fist
pumps against face.
We run. Wait

for the police who
never show up
while drunks try
to take us home.

"Hate Crimes Up by One-third in 2008," *Globe and Mail*, June 14, 2010.

Gay Christmas or Halloween

Doily Man, fighting perspiration
from tabletops, Oompa Loompa
doopity doop, a post-apocalyptic
1980s witch doctor is grabbing your
ass, there are forty-three sailors in the room and
it isn't fleet week, two lesbian
Mormons, a bag of coke and
straw asks if you would like
to take a snort, Lady Gaga, Lady Gaga
Lady Gaga, Lady Gaga, Lady
Diana, a series of costumes that
are not easily identified but
they each involve a jockstrap, I am dressed
as a visual poem
but only Billeh gets it and doesn't
think it's that funny, the Golden
Girls are drinking with the wardrobe
who has lost the lion and the witch
I'm not sure what you are, but the sweat
is dripping the makeup off your face
Michael is wearing a children's bee
costume again, with the baby face
that is freaking out the drag
queens, who are dressed as one another.
Murderer-granny-tranny drenched in blood keeps
grinding on ghosts, causing to blush,
a flannelled waistcoat, Tron, a stick
man, the paper-bag prince, Salvador Dalí Parton, zombie
Justin Bieber, and don't tell Mom
the babysitter's dead, you couldn't get past the cloud
she was grinding on the flying nun
someone is dressed as you
but you're not popular
so no one gets it.

M4M, Missed Connections

a found poem from Craigslist

u were wearing red t-shirt and sun glasses.
i was reading a magazine

I think we're on the same team.
You had today off ... was that a hint?

I saw you looking over at me twice
from across the street as we were going our separate ways.

I hope you read this..cuz you were adorable..
and i regret not saying hi to you...

I was the guy wearing the baige blazer
and blue jeans and smiled back at you.

i know this is rediculous...
how can i find the person i wanted here

I am so sorry that I didn't go.
Somehow I lost you before it was over.

How to Sell

Broad
shoulders
big
chest
abs
Adonis
V
pelvis
cut
puns
using
the
word
dick.

Busy Drag Queen

for Raye Sunshine

How those breasts grow to that size
is always up for discussion, a sunshine

smile, her dress drags to the
ground. Full eyebrows, full body, full

breasts, full attitude. She is busy, she
is busy, she is busy, no she cannot help

you, she's busy. She lures with a flick
of lips and winks, but what magic

trick does she use to make the breasts
so big? Hide-a-dick isn't anything new

but hide a dollar bill in between those
baby heads and make a wish

because it's the sun that's hard to
find in Vancouver, even just a Raye.

MSM: Looking for

Just wondering if there are any cute younger 5'11",
slim, Asian, clean, dd free, good looking,

cute young, married, cut, fit, 160 pounds,
jock, defined, safe type guys.

I'm married, white 5'11" 140lbs, look young,
not looking for reciprocation.

Too cold to be out, looking for someone
looking for hot stall fun or your place.

Looking for no femmes, no twinks, no girly-guys,
no fatties, no old guys, better 'NOT TO ASK'

You contact this dude in good faith,
then he asks for cash for smokes and booze.

Looking in cloverdale, looking
to host, looking for you.

If You Had

I don't think we could date if you had, if
you had, I would not think of having sex
with you at all, if you had, I would guess
you were a slut, if you had, I would even
feel scared about kissing you. If you had
would you go out to sex parties and drug
your last days? I bet he has, and had. Oh,
it should be fine. I bet you can't even get
from that. You only had three partners, so
they couldn't have given you, but say you
had, sure, then we'd work something out.
If you had, we would just switch to oral. I
heard you could get, from drinking a cup
of someone else's spit. I don't know how
he did it, especially when lying about not
having, and they still dated. Oh, if you had
and didn't tell me, I would kill you. If you
had, and kept it a secret, I would have you
arrested, well that's only even if you had.

He Wore Sequence

for Ron

The priest lays white cloth over his
coffin: let the cover slip down

like a dress, let bones sleep, let blood.
This cloth is for his confirmation

and this candle for baptism.
The purple is for mourning, the gold

is for hope, happiness only from heaven, sadness
on earth, sometimes happy, but mostly boring …

Ron sits next to me, says,
Holy, this gurl needs to get a life.

The priest lays white cloth over his wooden coffin
like setting a table. White cloth over

laugh, over bend and snap over
his faux drag name, La Fat Hoe.

The priest swings incense over his
coffin. The smoke rolls over

missed goodbye, over truth
over us, over the rainbow, somewhere.

The smoke brings his spirit up,
and no one can get him down.

He's on the dance floor, not in
a wooden frame. Ron sits next

to me, or above me, or with me
or in a wooden frame.

We sit back and let the sunlight catch
our sequence.

He wore sequence to shine
we let it glimmer in the sunset.

If Vancouver

If Vancouver and if recycle breathe of entitlement and if you micro- brew/micro hangover if hipsters could feel if three gunshot wound dead from leaky condo, if the heart is a stem and if one throws glass in rock houses on 4th and Balsam if a coffee cup bank account if a drug deal suburban McDonald's Double Cheeseburger Meal if for fuck's sakes if te-te-te-te-te-techno in Hummers bump bump bump off the dashboard, if you meet me at the corner of Davie and Burrard with a bat, if you can't sell this house, if a construction dating site on Stanley Park boat dock lovemaking if Oprah moves here I am going to literally shit my pants, if you add doot, doot dooloot doot to doot doot if you call home 1,235,000 dollars if we love you, if I am maybe attending or if I am not attending, but I am definitely not attending, if diuretic anxiety passing lanes of pedestrian pedagogy, if you are a car if you are a bike if you are a person, if you can't pay your rent, if art, if nature, if I forgot my umbrella again, if we are the ownership of death, if you have ever lost a loved one to Labrador lululemon leprosy call Sarah McLachlan right now, if I wanted to get married I very well could but the hell if I am, if you move to Victoria, if boomers would retire, if organic Mexican pepper avocado swine flu penicillin shots at the bar, if STI check-ins before the party, if you really thought I was checking my Twitter, actually I was texting you back to check out what I updated on my Twitter, if you're afraid to leave your apartment, if my coffee isn't extra hot again I am going to totally lose my shit, if I walk down the street and you hold my hand, if you could just tell me if I'm offended by this that would be great, if raw diet, if ironic moose-wool sweater, if anything, if the world is watching, if you forgot your keys again, if no you're stupid, no you're stupid, no you're stupid, if I appropriate your culture will you appropriate mine, if this coffee shop can build my career as an intellectual, if I write that novel, only if I get that grant, if that's racist, if you're homeless, if you could spare some change, even just a little, if chronic nostalgia was proof that we did it all wrong.

Three Blocks from Beach Avenue

i told them   we with our technologee n
entertainment n compewtr science have
lost th reeson evn for valid short term
mating n sumtimes think we have evolvd
byond needing it but not reelee from
wanting sum romance   can gees go cruising
— bill bissett, "i was on beech avenue in vancouvr"

I

He tells you, *It's nothing I can control,*
heavy breaths in the car that sweats windows
wets lips, wets eyes. Last time condensation
hit the window this hard, you were bent over
your ex, to be caught by the neighbour and
his dog. Now your heart is pressing against
the window and not your salivating
mouth. He needs more and you can't deny it
feels all too familiar. Tell the truth, you
want to do this too, you can't imagine
this, you, him staying the course without your
boat docking in more than just one port. But
can your bodies handle the dissection?
Open might mean open for infection.

II

Open might mean open for infection
but rest well with imaginings. Imagine
he goes out one night and has a bit too
much to drink and you've been gone away so
long he sees a man who talks a funny
talk and they make jokes with whatever they
can. They joke buttons and zipper undone
they joke the pants and shirt on the ground, they
joke the licks and taste of his skin, they joke
the sucking of cock, they joke inside of
him, they joke kisses, tongue, flesh, sweat the bed
they finish without you, turn off the light
and you cannot help but hear them talk at night.

III

And you cannot help but hear them talk at night
whisper, smirk, a side glance, and say, *He fucked
him, you know*, eye roll, quick flip of leg, hand
covers mouth from view, *they had a third in
the bedroom, and I am just waiting for
disaster*, looks left, cough the name up, *have
you heard, they don't even sleep together
anymore*, looks right, *not there* and he was
and a time-ticking self-deconstruct
mode waiting to happen, a smug grin, but
the truth is, you have heard it all before
it is only a used rubber on the floor.

IV

It is only a used rubber on the floor
dirty towel, folded inside itself
so as not to get anything on the bed
a bed, the phone on silent, the K-Y
the unfamiliar lamplight, taps of rain
at the window trying to calm your nerves, empty
bottles of wine, napkins for spills, two shot
glasses, the sweat of slippery feet, now
cold, as you trip over sleeping books, slip
out the door. You left your socks, half a six-
pack and the weak explanation you would
tell him. Frantically press the Down button
your finger feels numb. You can recall that
saying, you lose a piece of yourself each time.

V

Saying, *You lose a piece of yourself each time,*
so that whenever he goes off, you know
he will come back without something. He gave
his arms to the two from Kelowna, his
legs to the bartender, lost his knees in
Seattle, he gave his spine to his ex.
His eyes haven't been there since the man from
Brazil came along. You gave your shoulders
to the guitarist, you know this because
he weighs heavy on them. Ten years from now
all that will be is your arms, his baby toes
and your elbows, in twenty years, it will
be unseen, except for sounds of heartbeats
and a soft rustling where the skin meets.

VI

And a soft rustling, where the skin meets
causes an electric shock, you wake up
and can hear him crying, *I can't*
see you. So you turn on the lights but you
laugh when he cries so you think of
serious things, think of sad babies and
people dying. *Remember that talk we*
had? Is that all right with you? You smile
the conversation closed and pull the night
over his body, paint the stars back
in the Vancouver sky. *Everything is*
fine, he smiles and lets one rip into
the sheets, and you laugh into his chest as
he tells you, *It's nothing I can control.*

Mommie Dearest

for Jaylene Tyme

When we walk in the night, you quiet
yourself. Not like any drag queen I've ever
met. Shy and polite, nibble words
like you don't want to get the crumbs
on your dress. When the chandeliers
are hung, the drapes are holstered
to your shoulders, I can see you for the first
time, and you have a *Don't fuck with me,*
fellas! This ain't my first time at the rodeo
attitude that sprays words that hit
back walls and slide to the floor.
I was driving home when someone corrected
me – you were playing Faye Dunaway and not
Barbra Streisand. There are so many things
you have yet to teach me, oh mommie dearest.

Alphabet

e is for I love you, you feel good inside, all-night sex, this burrito
tastes terrible but the grass feels amazing, let's not go back to Oasis,
and let's head to Numbers because I know someone who has some
more of it, then head to the World, but leave your boyfriend behind
because he's sober as fuck and falls asleep by three. Roy? Yes, Roy will
help you with another hit. Jaw clench, teeth grinding, hard tab hit.
House party dress-up and it's wearing off so that bunny costume is
pretty fucked up and I can't deal with the three-day depression. Eat a
banana.

k is for I don't even know what this party is about anymore, can you take me home and let's have sex I just need to get out of this hole first. Sugar on my tongue and I can finally find my body again, I thought I left it at the coat check but it ended up on the second floor of Celebrities making out with my cousin.

ghb is for thirteen missed text messages, blackout, blackout, blackout, can't remember anything that happened last night, can you?

lsd is for get me out of here, this bear is touching me and the light is artificial. I want English Bay, fresh fruit, Stanley Park on my back and I can tell you about the first time I made love, but I can't wipe this smile from my face. I'll be more in love with you tomorrow.

pcp is for I miss my family.

mdma is for ya. ya. ya. ya. ya. ya. ya. ya. ya. ya. ya. aw now I'm sleepy.

hcl is for nose tingles, and don't take it from him, or else you'll be shitting in the stall. Let me call my guy, and I just need to dance a bit. I know I'm sweating, you don't need to fucking tell me. What was that? What was that? And. I. Can. Do. Anything. And. I. Am. Not. Tired. One more line. One more line. One more line. One more line. One more line. One more line.

The Rabbit Hole

the World after-hours

Holding up the wall
with the weight of his body

With eyes shut
mumbles in sleep

He's probably in a g-hole
so the bouncer brings a Coke

sips of sugar don't work
he still can't find his body

You hear the faint sound
of *Help me* and call

the ambulance. You send
him off and continue

the night as Granville shuts down
You think you know how

to party but are humbled
one hour later, seeing the man

who was sent off to the
ambulance, snorting a rail

hospital wristband
dangling from arm.

It's Taut, Part II

Call the ambulance to
get the vodka bottle
out of his neck, he
can't stop the bleeding
until the baseball bat
stops rushing to
his body, he never
liked that sport anyway.
The lead
pipe can't help you
now, it's cutting, gashing
into the back of your
head. Use this concrete
and bite down hard
to stop the bleeding
out of your teeth, gums
wound, sore, cold without
your clothes. Take
this knife and use
it to sew the skin
back together or use
my teeth to bite
safety on your ass. If
you can't scream for
help, then get a rope
from the store and
rent a hotel room for
the night. Make sure
it's taut
around your neck
just like I taught you
earlier.

GTL or Gym Tan Laundry

for that guy who waxes his armpits

There used to be this
steam room in the Davie gym
but they shut it down.
They found out what all the extra
steam was from. Is it the gays or
the gaze?
        This ab-workout video
didn't work in two weeks. He's
hot, but his face is weird, butter face or
bucket head. He was orange by
the time summer came. Leather
hide-like, his wrinkles smoothed
by BOTOX. I wax everything
including the armpits, feel how
smooth. He's got gay face, no
that looks more like stank face.
He
switched to brown linen.
No
one said gay sex was
going to be easy. Spray tan
the winter off your body. I can't today
it's a gym day.
        Sometimes I stare
at the wash cycle without blinking, I
can see into the future. I want a bigger
chest, we must, we must, we must increase
our bust. He's a silver daddy, but
not a sugar daddy. I'm just not built for
relationships
I'm built Tom Ford tough. They
used to have a steam room
in the Denman gym, but now
you wait outside Steamworks
pretending to wait for buses
that never come.

How to Sell, Part II: Lube, Booze and Cruise

Growl Fridays where Boys will be boys or sometimes girls. Careful, Hot
boy dancing on
the bar nightly. Stay and play specials.
You stay, you pay. You break, you buy. Did you bring your fake
ID Glide
Lube? Student & Active Military five-dollar all-day breakfast. Senior
Sundays at Squirt, Get a taste for free. Where the men stay
but the clothes leave without tipping. Being Wreck
Beached. Clothing is forever optional.

Thanks, Coach, or What Gay Porn Has Taught Me

I joined the soccer team because Coach
always teaches a lesson. Swimming pools

encourage gay sex. College guys love college for the hazing, which
is why you were so popular in second year.

Every businessman is hiding an erection, a gay agenda and a wedding ring.
Every straight roommate is waiting for a gay threesome.

It doesn't matter if he has a girlfriend. Gangstas have crazy sex parties
which is why you tattooed *thug passion* on your back.

He was straight until he passed out, or his girlfriend doesn't know, or
he was given four hundred dollars or he got on the bus.

The plumber is here, and he's going to fix more
than your leaky faucet. One must always wear a jockstrap,

even at times when it is completely unnecessary.
That's not how a doctor inspects your prostate.

Detention is where you have sex with your teacher
but prison is where inmates and guards make love.

Pumpjack, Part II: Sunday

Leather cap studs the collar. The
motor of his wheelchair buzzes the room.

These eight-dollar pitchers taste like shit. Papier-mâché
dick hangs over the pull-tab station, looms

as if it will drip down and slink off the wall. He rides over
discarded pull tabs, peanuts, unopened condom packages.

All the single ladies.
All the single ladies.

He stares down the urine trough filled with ice. The smell
of bleach and draft. Piss on the rocks.

He tweaks the nipples of memory, pinches yesterdays
chokes the *I remembers* in leather-strapped dreams.

I'm Doug and this is my boyfriend, Steven.
You're cute and we're about to go home.

He sips chilled draft, lips a sigh that rolls until
the end of the room, watches the men, watches the men.

You've got a little something on your nose. Pencils
in the Keno number, circling eleven.

He rides his Rascal to the end of the night. Sees
the spanked-bum pink sunset of tomorrow.

Rides over the years, stays in between the wrinkles
of his face, the sex-swings of his past.

How to Sell, Part III: Bearly Legal

Bear Bar, come see what all
the fuzz is about. Did you
laser hair removal, back,
torso, genitals buttocks
to Bear, Bath & Beyond?
Bottoms: a consistent top
choice. Clean is the new dirty.
Two's company, three's Excess
or a Mantourage. Banana
Video Come on up and peel
one some time! Inn Leather.
The Affordable INN place
for Out men. Cub Scrub
body soap you made him
act dirty, now help him get
clean. Work out, hang out,
make out. Out in style. You're
using the out door to enter.
RAM bookstore, leave your
inhibitions at home, movies,
lubes, toys accessories,
LATE NIGHT ACTION,
Magazines, VHS tapes Back
Room, Sink all the balls in 55
seconds or less, Win $100.
Please enter through the rear.

Walmart

It's a bit early in the day for vodka, but he calls, and there's not much to do, so they search the Internet, blog by blog. "People of Walmart." Baggy pants, tight tops, cut-off jeans, 1980s, vintage, half-Santa-suits. By 3 p.m., they dress. Walmart attire, slip into tank tops too big, too small, pants too old, *this will be so funny*. Rail lines off the dashboard. Grab the *oh-shit* bar as they try to stay in between the lines. Pull up to VPD, play it cool play it straight, play Lady Gaga on the system. Cocaine calls, too late to turn back. $13.99 credit-card cuts. They run through the aisles. Eat cereal from the box. Prices and their eyes roll back, can't get *te-te-te-te-telephone* out of their heads. Credit card swipes. Bags under their eyes, bags of Lay's, bags of reduced-price Halloween decorations. Apartment haunted by plastic ghosts.

The Odyssey

It wasn't long before your shirt was gone.
Snapping
shoulder back like runway clicks
like runaway hits, like hissy fits
in the middle of the dance floor.
I will not
call you my daddy. I don't
even call my dad … Daddy.
Leathered persistence.
You're super cute. I'm seeing someone –
Get over yourself, you're not that cute.
Vaseline
on the muscular and lean. Isn't
that your uncle? He's your uncle too.
He can come in, but he'll have to pay.
Didn't they play that Janet Jackson song three
times already? Yeah, but nobody noticed. Cocaine
on toilet seats.
Just use the fucking urinal. Sweat
are you okay? You're standing like a backslash.
Why is everyone leaving?
It's
last call.
But they haven't played
that Janet Jackson song yet.

It's Taut, Part III

for the Surrey School Board

These books are
not suitable for
the classroom.

These books are
not suitable for
the classroom.

These books are
not suitable for
the classroom.

These books are
not suitable for
the classroom.

These books are
not suitable for
the classroom.

These books are
not suitable for
the classroom.

These books are
not suitable for
the classroom.

These books are
not suitable for
the classroom.

These books are
not suitable for
the classroom.

These books are
not suitable for
the classroom.

These books are
not suitable for
the classroom.

These books are
not suitable for
the classroom.

These books are
not suitable for
the classroom.

These books are
not suitable for
the classroom.

These books are
not suitable for
the classroom.

These books are
not suitable for
the classroom.

These books are
not suitable for
the classroom.

These books are
not suitable for
the classroom.

These books are
not suitable for
the classroom.

Another West Side Story

for Cunty

I

Bludgeon face, the open palm
to nose, broke through, rose
drip on the dance floor. Take
flight, after kicks to the ribs

all because you wouldn't
dance with him, or date.
Took Denny's booth, and
you pigeon puffed chest

whispered, *Let's jump 'em
when they leave.* I respond
*No, I don't do gay-on-gay
crimes. We get beat enough.*

He begs me to fight, but
in my mind's eye, gays
dance fight, or turn it into a musical
West Side–like.

II

Revenge with bottle broken
and rouged from your
hand. This time from crushed
glass pressed between fingers.

Hold back his rage
with another beer
this one full, and cool
tempers with jokes.

When the bottle runs
clear, remember the
feeling of the sneaker
against your face.

Lose your shit, but know this:
cuts to his skin
are cuts to your own, even
if his nickname is cunty.

It's Taut, Part IV

The ████████ ███████ ████████ ████████ hate ████ ████ ████ ████████ ████ █████ ████ ████ had been walking hand in hand ████████ ████████ ████████ ████████ on a ████ ████████ broken. ████ ████ ████ ████████ ████ sentence ████████ ████████ ████████ ████ ████ ████████ ████ ████ ████ ████ ████████ ████ ████████ ████ ████ ████ ████ ████ ████ ████ ████ ████ ████████ ████ ████ ████ ████ two men holding ████ ████ ████ ████ ████ ████████ Canada, ████ ████ ████ ████ choose, ████ heterosexual ██ ████ ████ ████ ████ obligations, ████████ ████ ████ ████

██████████████████████████████████
████████ he said as he realized ████████████████████████
████████████████████████████████
his ████
████████████████████████ sentence ████████████████
████████
████████████████ would be ████████████ about ██████████
██████
████████████████████████████████ love ████████
████████████████ not ████████████████████████
████████████
██
████████████████████████████████, hatred.
"Those who act like he ████████ did ████████████████
must know ████████████████████████████████
████████████████████
██
████████ guilty████████████████████████████████
████████████
██
████████████████████████████████████ West
End.
██
████████████████████████████████
█Faggots██What the fuck is this████████████████

men what

submission

was assaulted, was bullied

he

██████████████, ████████ ████████████, ████████ ████████, had his jaw wired shut and suffered a concussion.

████████████████████████████████ was unconscious on the ground ██ ██ ████████████████████ threatened to "do him in."

██ homophobic language was ████████████████████████████████, ████████ ████████████████████ the punch ████ thrown. Therefore, ██ ████████████████████████ hate ████████

████████ disagreed.

██ ██ ████████████████████████████████ hate ████████, ██████ said ██ language was used before ████████████████████████████, ████ ██ ██ ████████████████████████████, and that no alternate explanation was available.

He ██ ████████████

██ ██ began to pass sentence. ███ knowledge███ would have ██████████ no ███████ sentence.

"I apologize," ██████████████████████████████████████ ████ "I am ██████████████████████████████████ ████████████ gay ██████."

███████████████████████████████ "I'd like to believe ███ hope ████████████████," he added.

██ ████████████████

██ imposing sentence█████████ noted the offence ████████ ████████████████████████████████████ ████████████████████████████ █████████████████████████████████████ █████████

██ including the ████████████████████████████████████ ██████████████████████████████████████ ████████ young. You have time to change your ways█ ████████████████████████████████ to turn your life around█

Little Sisters

So be a girly man
& sing this gurly song
Sissies & proud
That we would never lie our way to war
— CHARLES BERNSTEIN, "The Ballad of the Girly Man"

That we would never lie our way to war
or slit the throats of men
or strangle the world with
our oil. Hell yeah, we are

sissies & proud
of it, goddammit.
Your son may have come
home wearing a dress
like Carrie Bradshaw, but
did he burn the flesh of
men? So get up on that stage

& sing this gurly song
because this ain't gangsta rap
and the Pussycat Dolls never
put a man in a state of rage, well
maybe that one time.

So be a girly man
and put on your press-on
nails, streak your hair, put
a bow tie around your neck
and, girl, you better work.
Because it may offend their eyes, but
remember: the only war
we wage is on the dance floor
or in men's hearts.

How to Sell, Part IV: We're Open

Sex shop, gay cruising club, jockstrap & Internet access. WiFight it?
This Ramrod, Machine has Sling room, gang showers, Dungeons and
Dragons, Dark Room with maze, and Full Juice Bar available, in case
you get thirsty. Amateur strip shows start with nightly drink specials
until you've loosened up a bit. Live entertainment & shows, sexy man
contests, Karaoke or unsexy man contests. 100 rooms, 100 lockers,
steam room, dry sauna whirlpool, XXX movies, Glory Holes, Dark
rooms, dimly lit rooms, no ugly lights, Massage, and foam party. Think
High School Musical, but with blow buddies, m4m, slings and jail cells.
8 Times The Fun, Free HIV and STD testing. Private viewing booth.
Peep shows are so 20th century.

Plenty of Fish Dot-com

for the guy who mistook the garbage bin for a bear

Profile pictures of
hi and :)
         Wait for response
Make a joke about how hard it is to meet guys online
                I watch a lot of MTV Canada
                That's not what criterion means
IM: *Hi. What are you up to?*
I never trust anyone who uses the tongue-out smiley face.
         What's Friendster?
             don't worry, it doesn't have to be a "date,"
I only go on dudesnude to see who I know.
            txtd *I'm already seeing someone* translation
            I drank two pitchers liked you.
            you're sweating a lot.
            sorry, I've never been on a date with a guy
       before.
       Weed as recreation, *but how do you get the feta to be*
       dry like it is on the salads?
He was married with two kids, but now he is
               gay, single and ready to mingle,
         don't worry, the divorce is happening.
     IM: *I was just on MSN and you were on Manhunt, did you*
block me?!?!
          I really wish they had Choose Your Own
       Adventure for adults.
           Isn't that what this is.
Don't tell him he's bad in bed, just say it's because you don't like his
haircut
       that's not a bear, that's a garbage bin.
Don't forget the kiss at the end of the date and
someone will always tell you there are
plenty of fish
in the sea.

Vancouver, After the Rain

after Brad Cran and Gillian Jerome
for Lee Cote

It knocked at the window
and you didn't let it in. You complain
about how they painted the clouds the
wrong colour
you complain they painted the
clouds at all, but the wash
left grey paint all over
the concrete. Flyers and signs
gather at the sewer drain and
put a cast around the corner
like the time you broke your
ankle. You drained English Bay and
carried it in a bucket to the shore
where the sand sealed. You
collected the doors to hang, left
the cars for insects.
When the time came, you packed
your short-shorts, sailor hat
the past, a book for reading and brought
a six-pack to drink the ride.
You and me, we jumped
in the U-Haul, drove east until
I felt easy. It rains here too, but
someone painted the clouds purple
and the rain spreads his ashes
even though we never asked him to.
For a brief moment, you thought
it was sunny, but that was just me
painting the sky a different colour.

Walt Whitman Doesn't Even Drink Here Anymore

translation for Garry Thomas Morse

It is what it is, I already figured
you were in love with another man

or the likeness of, but it's like
how most gay men I know

can translate any quote
recited from *Mean Girls*, how

come you never txtd me back?
We never met because you

hadn't updated your status. So
here is Davie, & Starbucks.

We met one time, I was
drunk on vodka, wearing a

sailor hat, & you put your
number in my cellphone

but I blacked out the conversation
the erasure of our beginnings.

My skinny latte has whipped cream
on top. I was there

but there was no one in the library.
So you agree, you think you're really pretty?

I can't afford to be in Pride
this year. & you sigh every time

he walks into the room. Doom
& gloom is kind of your thing.

But this is Safeway.
Sorry, sir, this is Shoppers Drug Mart.

I bought the plastic corn because
I thought it would be funny & we could laugh

but you brought him up again. & I see
the lines on your wrist. He's waiting for you.

I wish it was just D&G & you & me, but
harmony is just a girl's name.

You have more than thirteen items.
I know, but I'm in an express hurry.

I've been staring at you in the
kitchen aisle, & you're not

sure if Bounty will quickly
pick up your mess, or if the no-name

brand will work
just the same, & I watch you

but who will watch me watching
you. When my boyfriend

reads this, he will tell me he
likes it better when I write the poems

that are funny, & I slip on
your glittery strap-on of dawn.

Tomorrow

Forever we push carts along dirt roads of counts in tomorrow, make birds into stones and move the rocks so that when they vibrate, they spring to life, make chickens, roasts, tomatoes that are too modified to produce organs.

Friday we walk the streets of rain and grey coats the bottoms of pant legs. We can't wash the grey out, we'll have to bleach our eyes and teeth again. Put the coin on my lips, I'll use it for the laundry later.

When you call I hear someone else speaking. The Scarecrow asking for his brains, the zombie requesting Facebook friendship, but my flesh has been devoured so I can only poke back with bones.

Forget the video-game men, square chests cut.

When the government came asking for money, I apologized and said I had no change left. I only use debit.

I followed you, falsely.

When we wear our costumes, you have birds flocking you, landing on the tips of your fingers. When I stick my fingers out, they pick the nails or ignore friend requests.

You have one mutual friend with yourself.

Saturday we boil our guts with beer and call for cabs that will take us to cabs. You'll recount the wine that has stained your skin and I'll recount the ways. When we arrive at the ocean, we find it empty again. Someone flushed the earth and seaweed lays dried like flowers for death.

I had a career in careerism until I lost it all when the precession hit.

When you call, I can hear my mother's voice, she asks for flour. I can't quite eat the pie or else my irritable bowel will talk about the time he quaked the silos.

Or this is just another poem about you.

Saturday, we couldn't get past, it just went on and on. When all the Fridays and Thursdays died off, we couldn't find any more bars to drink. We just sat at the beginning of Saturday hoping the sun would set to make way for Sunday, but Sunday called in terminally sick or had to take permanent stress leave. Annie is still singing about tomorrow.

If I close my eyes I see the world in which would have been – had you the ability to regenerate body. I fail and fail and fail, at least this world has your hands.